HEALING

Participant Journal

THE WOUNDED HEART

HEALING
THE WOUNDED HEART

Participant Journal

Trauma Healing Institute

HEALING THE WOUNDED HEART: AN INMATE JOURNAL
SECOND PRINTING

© 2018 American Bible Society

ISBN 978-1-58516-127-0-a
ABS Item 124735

Adapted by Dana Ergenbright and Joy Stevens
from *Healing the Wounds of Trauma*
© 2009, 2013, 2016 Harriet Hill, Margaret Hill, Richard Baggé, and Pat Miersma
in partnership with Good News Jail and Prison Ministry (goodnewsjail.org)

This book is intentionally written in basic English.

Unless otherwise noted, Scripture quotations are taken from the *Good News Translation® (Today's English Version, Second Edition)* © 1992 American Bible Society. All rights reserved. Passages marked **CEV** are from the *Contemporary English Version®* © 1995, 2006 American Bible Society. Bible stories are adapted from Scripture. Passages marked **NLT** are from the *Holy Bible, New Living Translation*, copyright © 1996, 2004, 2015 by Tyndale House Foundation. Used by permission of Tyndale House Publishers Inc., Carol Stream, Illinois 60188. All rights reserved.

Editor: Peter Edman
Design: Jordan Grove
Illustration: Ian Dale
Set in Post Grotesk.

For training in how to use this book to carry out trauma healing, see your local Bible Society, visit TraumaHealingInstitute.org, or write to traumahealing@americanbible.org.

Trauma Healing Institute

101 North Independence Mall East FL8
Philadelphia PA 19106-2155

CONTENTS

Welcome	7
If God loves us, why do we suffer?	9
How can the wounds of our heart heal?	19
What happens when someone is grieving?	33
Taking your pain to the cross	45
How can we forgive others?	53
Looking back	63
On your own	67

WELCOME

Introduction

💬 DISCUSSION

What are your hopes for this group?

In this group, we'll be talking about the wounds of our hearts. Each lesson is interactive, and you may feel uncomfortable emotions at times—perhaps anger, sadness, anxiety, irritability, or tenseness. This is normal. It's part of the healing process, because we can't *heal* until we *feel*.

But you can choose if you want to participate and how much you are willing to share with others.

💬 DISCUSSION

What should be the ground rules for our group?

The healing journey

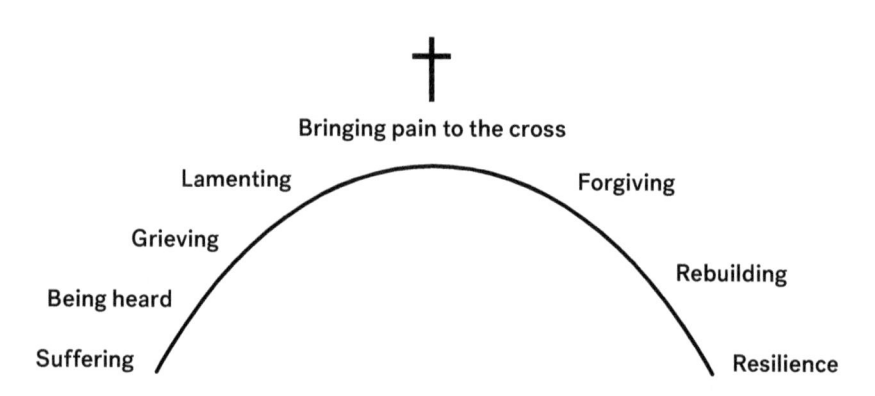

✝

Bringing pain to the cross

Lamenting   Forgiving

Grieving

                                     Rebuilding

Being heard

Suffering   Resilience

When people experience suffering and loss, their hearts can be wounded. For these wounds to heal, people need to express their pain to someone who listens to them without causing further harm. They need to accept the pain of the loss and grieve so that those feelings are not buried alive inside them. They can express these feelings honestly to God in lament. Once identified and expressed, they can bring that pain to Christ, who died on the cross for sin and everything sin brought with it: death, pain, sickness, conflict, abuse, and so forth. As we experience Christ's healing, we come to a place where we can begin to forgive those who have hurt us. We can begin to rebuild our lives and communities. We are better able to face suffering in the future.

IF GOD LOVES US, WHY DO WE SUFFER?

1. The story of Ben

Ben grew up in the city of Las Palmas. He never knew his father. Until he was three, he was raised by his mom. Then she died and he had to go live with his aunt. Her husband was cruel to Ben. He beat Ben often and didn't give him enough to eat.

Ben went to school and made friends. When he was in middle school, one of his friends invited him to his church. Ben believed that Jesus had died for him, so he became a Christian. The church became like a family to him, and with the support of the pastor's family, Ben graduated from high school and got an associate's degree in substance abuse counseling. When he was just twenty-two, he got a job as an addictions counselor at a clinic in a town nearby. He got married and had two sons.

Over the years, gangs began to take control of his neighborhood in Las Palmas. Rival gangs had huge fights nearly every week. Ben saw innocent people being shot—children, women, passersby. Several of the young girls in his church had been gang raped. Other families were robbed at gunpoint. Las Palmas had become a war zone.

Ben was leaving work one day when he got the dreaded call: come to the emergency room! His five-year-old son Johnson had been hit by a stray bullet. By the time Ben got to the hospital, it was too late. The doctors were not able to save little Johnson's life.

Ben still goes to church and believes in the Bible, but he keeps asking why God has let him and his community suffer. He is angry with God and feels that God has deserted him. He has a hard time praying and his heart feels dead toward God. When he thinks of God as his Father, he can't imagine a loving father. In his experience, he only knew a father who was absent and an uncle who beat him cruelly.

One day he began to think of what he had been taught at school—that God didn't exist, that God did not create the world. Ben knew that this was not what the Bible teaches, but some part of him felt it might be true after all. Maybe there wasn't a God listening to his prayers.

Ben still takes his family to church and tries to teach his son about God, but he feels like a hypocrite because he talks about God's love, but he really feels God is far away.

DISCUSSION

1. What is Ben feeling in his heart about God?
2. Why do you think Ben feels this way?
3. Have you ever felt like Ben?

2. When we are suffering, what do we need to remember about God's character?

DISCUSSION

What does the culture tell us about God, especially in times of suffering?

GOD'S CHARACTER

Culture says ...	The Bible says ...
	Romans 8:35-39
	Psalm 34:18
	Genesis 6:5-6
	Matthew 9:35-36

Romans 8:35-39. God still loves us.
Sometimes when trouble comes we think it means God doesn't love us anymore. This is not true. Nothing can separate us from his love. God promises to always be with us, even when we suffer (Psalm 23:4-5; Hebrews 13:5b-6; Isaiah 43:1-2).

Psalm 34:18. God suffers with us and feels our pain.
Jesus understands our suffering because he suffered on the cross. His suffering was far beyond anything we will ever experience (Matthew 27:46; Hebrews 12:2-3). He suffers with those who are suffering (Matthew 25:35-36). He is merciful and gracious even when we have doubts (Isaiah 63:9; Isaiah 53:3-4; Hebrews 2:18).

Genesis 6:5-6. God hates evil and injustice.
Not everything that happens is the perfect will of God. God hates evil and injustice (Proverbs 6:16-19; Romans 1:18).

Matthew 9:35-36. Jesus looks for us when we are suffering and has compassion on us.
Jesus went looking for people who were suffering. He preached the Good News and healed people of all their diseases. He felt pity for them.

3. What is the origin of suffering in the world?

DISCUSSION

How do *you* think suffering came into this world?

The Bible tells us:
1. Satan rebelled against God, and he wants to get as many people as he can to rebel against God (1 Peter 5:8-9; John 8:44).
2. When Adam and Eve chose to disobey God, evil and death entered the world (Genesis 3:1-24; Romans 5:12).
3. God gives all of us the freedom to choose whether we will obey him or not (Matthew 23:37b; Romans 3:10-18; Matthew 7:13-14). Sometimes, even though we obey God, we suffer because of other people's choices (1 Peter 2:20-22; 3:14-17).

4. What other things can make it difficult to believe in God's goodness when we suffer?

Barriers	Biblical responses	Notes
If we only hear about God's anger and judgment	Jeremiah 31:3 Lamentations 3:22-23 1 John 4:9-11	
If we are told that suffering means we haven't done enough to please God	Romans 5:8 Titus 3:4-6	
If we are taught that God promises prosperity for everyone who believes	Philippians 1:29 1 Peter 2:21 2 Corinthians 1:8-10	
If we do not do the things that will help our faith grow strong	John 8:31-32 2 Timothy 3:14-17 Acts 2:42 Hebrews 10:24-25	
Childhood experiences that make it difficult to believe in God's goodness	John 17:24 Romans 8:14-17 1 John 3:1	

💬 DISCUSS IN PAIRS

Think about your own father. As a child, did you experience his love? Consider the same with your mother. How does your experience with your earthly parents affect your experience with your heavenly Father?

If we only hear about God's anger and judgment.
It is true that God is all-powerful and judges sin, but we must also remember his great love for us (Jeremiah 31:3; Lamentations 3:22-23; 1 John 4:9-10).

If we are told that suffering means we haven't done enough to please God.
God's love is not based on our behavior. He loved us before we turned to him (Romans 5:8; Titus 3:4-5; 1 John 4:19). He continues to love us by grace, not because of what we do (Romans 3:23-24; Ephesians 2:8-9).

If we are taught that God promises prosperity for everyone who believes.
If we are taught that people who obey God will always be rich and healthy, we may feel guilty for suffering. We may feel that we have caused our own suffering by our lack of obedience and faith. The apostle Paul is a good example of someone who suffered a lot even though he was very obedient to God (2 Corinthians 1:8-10).

If we do not do the things that will help our faith grow strong.
As we follow Jesus and study the Bible, we learn the truth about God and this sets us free from the lies of Satan (John 8:31-32; 2 Timothy 3:14-17). Christians need to meet together for teaching, prayer, and fellowship (Acts 2:42; Philippians 4:6-7; Hebrews 10:24-25). If these things are missing, we will find it much harder to believe in God's goodness when we suffer.

Childhood experiences that make it difficult to believe in God's goodness.
Children need to feel secure and protected from evil. If we have experienced difficult things as a child, we may find it difficult to trust God when we become adults. For example, if we grew up without a father or mother, or if our father was often angry with us, then we may think God has abandoned us or that he is always angry with us, even though the Bible teaches us that God is a loving Father (John 17:24; Romans 8:14-17; 1 John 3:1).

» *Experiencing God's love*

It may be hard for you to receive love from God the Father because you view him through the lens of your earthly father. God our Father wants to give you pure and genuine love that will not hurt you in any way. Please receive that love as you reflect on these verses.

- **Lamentations 3:21–24.** *Yet hope returns when I remember this one thing: The LORD's unfailing love and mercy still continue, fresh as the morning, as sure as the sunrise. The LORD is all I have, and so in him I put my hope.*
- **1 John 3:1.** *See how much the Father has loved us! His love is so great that we are called God's children—and so, in fact, we are. This is why the world does not know us: it has not known God. My dear friends, we are now God's children, but it is not yet clear what we shall become. But we know that when Christ appears, we shall be like him, because we shall see him as he really is.*
- **Psalm 103:13.** *As a father is kind to his children, so the LORD is kind to those who honor him. He knows what we are made of; he remembers that we are dust.*
- **1 John 4:9–10.** *And God showed his love for us by sending his only Son into the world, so that we might have life through him. This is what love is: it is not that we have loved God, but that he loved us and sent his Son to be the means by which our sins are forgiven.*
- **1 Peter 5:7.** *Leave all your worries with him, because he cares for you.*

Taking care of yourself

When we start talking or thinking about the things we have experienced, we can begin to feel strong emotions. Remember, this is normal and is part of the healing process. There are many things we can do to take care of ourselves while we're healing.

» Breathing exercise

Breathing deeply can help us relax during strong emotions. If this makes you feel uncomfortable at any point, you can stop. You're in control.

- Get into a comfortable sitting position. (Later you can try this laying on your back.)
- Pick a spot on the wall and concentrate on it. Think only about your own breathing.
- Slowly breathe in and out, filling your lungs and slowly releasing the air. Imagine that you are pushing the breath to the wall and back. Think to yourself, "[Your name], feel yourself relaxing as oxygen is flowing in and out."
- Think about being in a quiet place. It might be the beach, or on a hill or in a tree. You might be alone or with someone who cares for you. You might think about Jesus telling you how much he loves you.
- Continue to think about your breathing, flowing in and out, in and out.
- After a few minutes, release your gaze from the spot on the wall. Stretch and take one more deep breath.

💬 DISCUSSION

Was this helpful to you? Why or why not?

Wrapping it up

What's one thing you want to remember from this lesson?

Voices

I came to this Jail, not knowing what is going to happen in life. I wanted to start praying to allow God back into my life. While i was here i tried to pray. But I couldn't because I was in this unit. There were only a few Believers. I've ask if anyone had a bible; no-one answer me. And when I was going to give up, I seen this Daily Bread, so i ask if this belong to anyone. No-one said a word. So i took it to my room. Like a new book to Read. I then ask my friend if i could use his Book. He said O.K., but i seen a bible on the countertop. I grab it, and went to my room again. And now I ask God to help me. And come back into my life. Now have someone to teach me. My prayer's were answer. I got to come to this place called God's Mod. My life started to change, I meet some special people there.

There was this little woman that had this glow that I seen. She came up and told us she was going to start a class and see needed guy's to attend it. I wanted to go but the line on the paper was long. Never though I was going to get pick. Though all the other people were going to get pick first because they were here way befor me.

My friend said, Hey we were pick. Are you going to go. I said yes I going to be in this History Event. So here i am. i was not expected to do alot in class. But I was ready for anything. I felt like a Black Kettle there not knowing what the class is about or how hot its going to get. And when it got hot all these's emotion started poping up. I was scared at first. Did any-one see that Bubble pop up. Cry's loud cry's I couldn't explain it. Because when they poped, the word's were writ on my face. I tryed to keep my head down, so that no one could read them. But the tear's started to flow out. And then the tears were washing all my word's from my face.

I feel alot better now, I can say it is time to move on, and I don't have to let my emotion strike to the bottom any more. Thank you God for allowing your Angel Joy come into my life's. I will be going to court for a while. I just got out of leavenworth, KS. I was there for awhile. I prayed in the Sweat Lodge. And I went to the church on ever other Sunday. I work in there M-F day's. Keep my life Busy and had the Lord and the Great Father in my life. Sorry I gave them both up when I got out. Now I have the Lord back in my life. Thank you God.

Voices

HOW CAN THE WOUNDS OF OUR HEART HEAL?

Taking care of yourself

Sometimes when we start thinking about the painful things we've experienced, we might feel like we're experiencing them again, like we're in the past rather than the present. When this happens, we can help ourselves by using our bodily senses to focus on the present moment.

» Senses exercise

Answer these questions in your mind, as a way to return yourself to the present.

- What are two things I can see?
- What are two things I can hear?
- What are two things I can feel?

Repeat the exercise, if needed, choosing additional things and describing them silently to yourself.

1. The fire

It was three in the morning when the phone rang in Laurel and Pete's bedroom. Laurel looked sleepily at Pete as he answered it, but became more alert as he started to get out of bed as he listened to the caller. "Bad fire," he said, "and it's coming this way!" Pete was a firefighter and Laurel was used to him being called out in the night, but somehow this seemed more serious than usual. Within five minutes Pete was out of the house on his way to the fire. Laurel wondered if she should wake the children, but first she went downstairs to turn on the television and find out what was happening.

Just as Laurel found a channel reporting on the fire, she heard cars driving outside, with loudspeakers telling everyone to get out. It took a while to get the three kids awake and dressed and into the car. As they left, clouds of smoke were getting nearer and they could even see the fire in the distance. Finally they arrived at a friend's house outside the danger zone. Laurel was so relieved to be safe, but then she began to worry about Pete.

There was no news for some hours but then Laurel got a message from a nearby hospital saying she should come at once because her husband was seriously hurt. As she rushed off, Laurel wondered if she would ever see Pete alive again. At the hospital, she heard that two other men in his unit had been killed and that Pete had burns on most of his body, his leg was crushed, and he had internal injuries. For three dreadful days, she thought he was going to die, but once they amputated his leg, he began to recover. It was a long time, though, before he could leave the hospital.

When he recovered, Pete was given a job in the office of the fire department. Laurel felt that things should be returning to normal but each week has seemed worse than the last. They both are having trouble sleeping and often have nightmares. But the worst part of it for Laurel has been Pete's personality change. Before the fire, he was generally a happy and balanced guy, but now he gets angry over little things. The children are beginning to be scared of their father because he yells at them when they make any noise. Laurel knows Pete is hurting inside because of the loss of his leg, but he won't talk about it because he thinks men should be strong. His friends just behave as though nothing has happened, but for Pete, his whole life has changed.

Laurel is becoming more and more depressed. She's lost interest in eating. It's especially hard for her at church because she is angry at God for not protecting her husband. Was God not able to protect him? Did God not care? What happened? Their pastor preaches that people who have strong faith in God are always H-A-P-P-Y and full of joy. Laurel knows this is not how she feels.

Finally Laurel talks to her small group leader, Pat. As she talks, she begins to cry and can't stop sobbing. It feels like pressure inside her has been released. Pat listens to Laurel tell what had happened. She asks Laurel to explain how she felt during the whole experience, and finally they talk about what the hardest part of the experience was for Laurel.

Laurel goes away feeling relieved. They have agreed to get together again for coffee the next week.

DISCUSSION

1. Besides the loss of Pete's leg, what else has he lost? What has Laurel lost? What do you think their children have lost?
2. In your area, what are some things people have lost?
3. What does your culture teach people to do with their emotions when they are suffering inside?

2. What is a wound of the heart?

Our hearts can be wounded when we are overwhelmed with intense fear, helplessness, or horror. This is referred to as trauma. It can happen in the face of death, serious injury, rape, or other forced sexual activity. Sometimes witnessing trauma can be just as difficult as experiencing it.

> **DISCUSSION**
>
> What are some sources of trauma? Consider those that are caused by humans as well as by nature.

> **DISCUSSION**
>
> How can incarceration contribute to trauma?

A heart wound is like a physical wound

> **DISCUSSION**
>
> Think of a physical wound. How does it heal? What helps it heal?
>
> How is a wound of the heart like a physical wound?

PHYSICAL WOUND	HEART WOUND
It is visible.	
It is painful and must be treated with care.	
It must be cleaned to remove any foreign objects/dirt.	
If a wound heals on the surface with infection still inside, it will cause the person to become very sick.	
Only God can bring healing, but he often uses people and medicine to do so.	

PHYSICAL WOUND	HEART WOUND
If not treated, it attracts flies.	
It takes time to heal.	
A healed wound may leave a scar.	

How do people with wounded hearts behave?

Proverbs 4:23 (NLT) tells us, *"Guard your heart above all else, for it determines the course of your life."* What happens to our heart affects how we live.

People with wounded hearts may behave in the following ways:
- **Reliving** the experience
- **Avoiding** reminders of the trauma
- **Being on alert** all the time

💬 DISCUSSION

Think about wounded people you know. Have you seen anyone acting in these ways? Have you ever acted in these ways? Explain.

How would these things make someone feel?

Reliving the experience

- thinking all the time about the event
- feeling like they're back in the event, while awake (flashbacks) or asleep (nightmares)
- telling everyone about what happened over and over again

This makes it hard to concentrate (i.e. at work or school).

Avoiding reminders of the trauma

- avoiding anything that brings back memories of event (i.e., places, people, emotions)
- going numb, not caring about what happens to them, not disturbed by violence or seeing dead bodies
- not remembering what happened, or only remembering parts of it
- using drugs or alcohol, or eating, working, or exercising too much, to avoid feeling the pain
- completely refusing to talk about it

Being on alert all the time

- always feeling tense, jumpy, frightened
- living in dread of another bad thing happening
- overreacting with violence or anger
- struggling to fall asleep, or waking up very early
- shaking, having a fast or irregular heartbeat
- having headaches and stomachaches
- feeling dizzy or faint, difficulty breathing, panic attacks

3. What does the Bible teach us about how to handle our feelings?

Some people who have troubles like these—even believers—say we shouldn't think or talk about our feelings. They say we should just forget the past and move on. They think that feeling pain in our hearts means we are doubting God's promises. This is not true! Here are some Bible passages that address strong feelings.

- Matthew 26:37-38 (Jesus)
- John 11:33-35 (Jesus)
- Matthew 26:75 (Peter)
- Jonah 4:1-3 (Jonah)
- 1 Samuel 1:10, 13-16 (Hannah)
- Psalm 55:4-6 (David)

Jesus had strong feelings and shared them with his disciples. Paul teaches us to share our problems with each other as a way of caring for each other (Galatians 6:2; Philippians 2:4). The Old Testament is full of examples of people pouring out their hearts to God. The writer of one psalm told God, *"I am hurt to the depth of my heart"* (Psalm 109:22). God wants us to be honest and speak the truth from our hearts.

💬 DISCUSSION

In your family, how do you handle emotions?

4. How can we heal from the wounds of our hearts?

One way we can begin to heal is by talking about our pain. Usually we need to talk to another person about our pain before we are ready to talk to God about it. We may need to tell our story many times. If we are able to talk about our bad experiences, then after a while our reactions will become less and less intense. But if we are not able to talk about our pain, and if there is no one to help us, these reactions may continue for months and even years.

A. What begins to happen when we talk about our pain?

When we talk with someone who knows how to listen:

- We can gain an honest understanding of what happened and how it has affected us.
- We can accept what happened.
- We can feel heard and know we are not alone.
- We can become able to trust and rest in God, and let God begin to heal our hearts (see Psalm 62:8 and Psalm 103:3).

B. What is a good listener like?

DISCUSSION

With what kind of person would you feel free to share your deep pain?

1. Creates a safe space

For us to share the deep wounds of our hearts with someone, we need to know that our listener:

- Cares about us.
- Will keep the information confidential.
- Will listen and understand our pain.
- Will not criticize us or give quick solutions.
- Will not minimize our pain by comparing it with their own pain.

2. Asks helpful questions

Here are three helpful questions to guide us when we are sharing our pain or listening to others:

- What happened?
- How did you feel?
- What was the hardest part for you?

3. Shows they are listening to us

- Looks at us, not out the window, at their watch, or at their phone.
- Doesn't seem impatient for us to finish.
- Says words of agreement like "Mmm."
- From time to time, repeats what they think we've said (so we can correct, restate, or affirm their understanding).

4. Respects the healing process

- Notices if we become very distressed and knows it's not helpful to continue. Lets us take a break, think about other things, and get calm inside. We can resume telling our story when we feel ready.
- May gently ask us if we would like prayer. If we say "yes," the listener prays but does not preach. If we say "no," the listener honors this.

» Listening exercise, in pairs

Talk about one bad thing that happened to you—a small thing, not the worst thing you've experienced. The other person listens, using the three questions above. Then switch roles.

Afterward, discuss these questions as a group:

- How did you feel during this exercise?
- Was anything difficult?
- Did you feel heard when you were listened to? Why or why not?
- What did the listener do well?

C. Serious cases

Certain things make heart wounds more serious ...

- Something very personal, for example, a family member dying or being betrayed by a close friend
- Something that goes on for a long time
- Something that happens many times over a period of time.
- Something connected with death
- Something that people have done intentionally to cause pain rather than something that is accidental

People react to painful events differently. Two people may go through the same event, but one may have a severe reaction while the other is not affected much at all. A person is likely to react more severely to trauma if he or she:

- always wants someone else to tell them what to do.
- has mental illness or emotional problems.
- is usually sad or is sensitive.
- had many bad things happen in the past, particularly if they happened when he or she was a child, like both parents dying.
- already had many problems before this happened.

» Art exercise

Another way we can get the pain in our hearts out without using words is by drawing. Start by getting quiet inside and asking God to show you the pain in your heart. Begin drawing one of your painful experiences without thinking about it too much. Try to let the pain come out through your fingers. The senses exercise and the breathing exercise can help you if you feel very strong emotions during this exercise.

💬 DISCUSSION

1. Share as much or as little as you'd like about your drawing. Or, if you'd prefer, share what the experience was like of drawing your pain.
2. Was there anything new you realized about your situation?

Taking care of yourself

Do the senses exercise and the breathing exercise before you leave.

What's one thing you will do to take care of yourself today?

Wrapping it up

What's one thing you want to remember from this lesson?

Voices

Oh God

Why do I continue to struggle with everything, why do I continue to loose the war Ive been fighting with my addictions to drugs and anger? Why do you not help me when I start to fall, Why do you seperate me and my family.

I love my family. I love my girl and my little girl so much and you took me away from them. Now I have to spend the rest of my life away from them. I wont get to see my children grow up. I wont get to teach my son how to be a man. I wont get to watch my daughter blossom in to a woman. My children will grow to hate me!

I ask you for mercy lord. I beg you for mercy in the court room.

I ask you to take this away from me God. I beg you please God let me be the father I need to be. Let me be the father my children deserve, even if your will is for me to raise my children from prison. God I trust and believe you are working in my life. God I trust in you and you are a god of mercy. I have never stopped believing that you are my lord and saviour. I have given my life to you, and I understand and have faith in your will, and your will will be done and I am fine with that.

Regardless of the outcome I will continue to praise you, I will continue to bring more and more of your sheep to you. I will stay in the word and spread your word lord. I love you lord

Love your Son

OPD Search warrant
Get on the Fu**ing ground now
Mommy Daddy!!!!
I'll Blow your head off
Leave her alone, Im Sorry
Im Sorry Baby mommy and Daddy Love you
I Love you Too Babe
I Love you ... we got this.

WHAT HAPPENS WHEN SOMEONE IS GRIEVING?

Taking care of yourself

Sometimes we can be overwhelmed by what we have experienced but we are not in a situation where we can express how we feel. This exercise can be helpful.

» *Container exercise*

Close your eyes or look down at the floor so you are not distracted. Imagine a big container. It could be a big box or a shipping container. Imagine a way to lock the container, like a key or a padlock.

Now imagine putting all the things that are disturbing you right now into the container: big things, small things—everything that is disturbing you. When they are all inside the container, close it. Now lock the container and put the key somewhere safe. Do not throw it away. When you are ready, open your eyes and look up.

Later, find a time when you can get quiet. Take the key and open the container, then one by one take out the things you have put inside. You may want to do this with someone who can help you talk about these things. Do not leave them in the container forever!

1. The night that changed Tony's life

Tony was home with his family after a long day at school and work. He lived on the "bad" side of town—if you weren't from there you would never go there, except by accident. Tony lived in a cramped one-bedroom apartment with his two younger brothers and his mom. He had goals to get his GED and help his mom raise his brothers. He worked hard to stay out of trouble and to avoid the gangs that so many of his friends had joined.

One night Tony took an extra shift at the pizza place where he worked, so he didn't get off until 11 p.m. The busy corner where he lived was on the line dividing two opposing gangs in his neighborhood. They were continually fighting for control of this neutral street.

On this night, a terrible battle broke out right in front of Tony's house. His mom was on her way home from picking up his brothers and they found themselves in the middle of it. His youngest brother was shot and killed immediately, and Joe, his other brother, was seriously wounded and taken to the hospital.

Tony came home to see police tape on the scene, and police everywhere. His neighbor got to him first and told him what happened. Tony ran toward the house, pushing wildly through the crowd. When a police officer tried to stop him, Tony punched him. The officer cuffed him, wrestled him to the police car, and booked him on assault.

In the jail, Tony's grief began to overwhelm him. He found himself crying when no one was looking. This made him feel embarrassed and he tried hard to hold in his feelings. He began losing sleep and was tormented with thoughts of guilt and regret. "If only I had been there, I could have stopped it!" Over and over again these thoughts ran through his mind. He also began to plot revenge on the gang members who had destroyed his family.

Because he had not been sentenced he was not able to furlough to his brother's funeral. He felt enraged at everyone—the officer who arrested him, the gang members, the attorney for not arranging a furlough, God for letting all this happen. When he didn't feel enraged, he felt numb, like he was walking through fog. "I can't believe this is happening to me."

💬 DISCUSSION

1. What has Tony lost?
2. What are some things you have lost as a result of being incarcerated?

2. What is grieving?

Grieving is feeling the loss of something.

💬 DISCUSSION

What kind of losses can we grieve?

Grieving is part of the normal process of recovering from loss. When we lose someone or something important to us, we may also lose a sense of who we are. As we grieve, our sense of who we are gradually changes and we adjust to our new stage of life. This takes time.

When Adam and Eve sinned, death came into the world—and with it the need for grieving. Only in heaven will there be no more pain and grief (Revelation 21:4).

3. How can we grieve in a way that brings healing?

The grief journey
Grieving takes time and energy. It is like a journey that requires stops at several camps, but leads to healing (Isaiah 61:1-3).

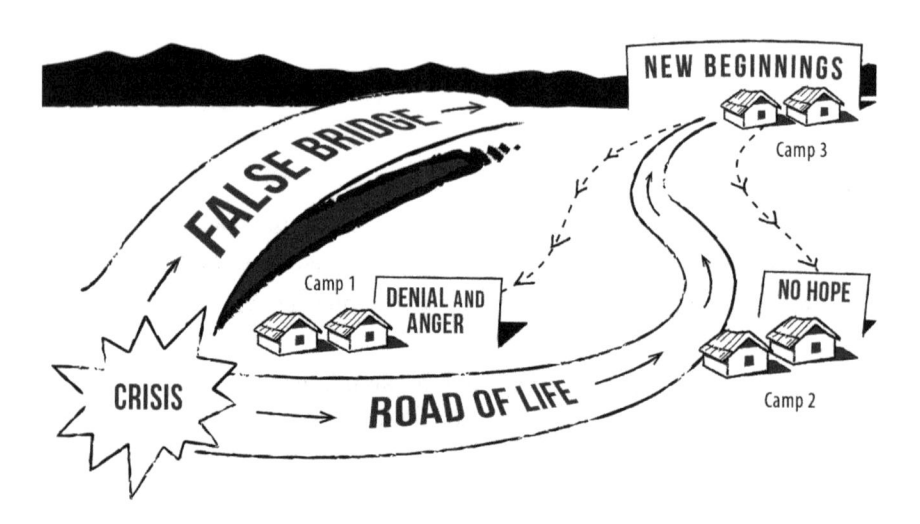

Camp 1: Denial and Anger

- Numb
- Not aware of what is happening around us
- Can't believe the person has died or the event has happened
- May suddenly start to cry or erupt in anger
- May be angry with God
- May be angry with a person who has died, for leaving us alone
- "If only I had done this or that, the person wouldn't have died" or "I wish I had …"
- "Why did this happen to me?"
- May find someone to blame for the death
- May take revenge, which results in conflict and more pain
- May think we hear or see the dead person

Camp 2: No Hope

- Sad and hopeless
- Hard to organize life
- Long for the dead person to come back
- May feel lonely
- May want to kill ourselves
- May feel guilty even if there is no reason to

Camp 3: New Beginnings

- Think about moving on to a new life
- Ready to go out with friends and have fun
- May consider remarrying if a spouse died, or having another child if a child died
- Changed by the loss; may be stronger, more tender

Backtracks and the 'false bridge'

The grief journey is not always direct. It is normal for people to revisit previous camps for a short period of time. Sometimes this happens in response to an event like the anniversary of a death.

It is tempting to try to bypass the process of grieving. We want to start over without dealing with our feelings about our loss, but this is not healthy. The grief will stay inside us and cause problems for many years. The **"false bridge"** is a dead end.

DISCUSSION, IN PAIRS

1. Think of a loss you have experienced. How would you describe that time?
2. In your grief journey, have you looped back or gotten stuck along the way? Explain.
3. Have you tried to take the false bridge to avoid feeling the pain of loss? Explain.

4. What can make grieving more difficult?

The type of loss

- When there are too many deaths or losses at the same time
- When the death or loss is sudden and unexpected
- When the death or loss is violent
- When there is no body to be buried or no way to confirm that the person has died
- When the person that provided for the family has died
- When we had unresolved problems with the dead person
- When the death is a suicide or murder
- When a child has died

Cultural beliefs about weeping

DISCUSSION

What does your culture or family think about men weeping? What does it say about women weeping?

Culture and weeping

- If our culture or family doesn't allow us to cry, we'll hold our grief inside rather than letting it out.
- God has designed us to cry or weep when we are sad. It's an important part of grieving, for men as well as women.
- Even Jesus wept when his close friend Lazarus died (John 11:33-38a). The psalmists wept (Psalm 6:6; 39:12; 42:3), as did the prophets (Isaiah 22:4; Jeremiah 9:1). Ecclesiastes 3:4 says there is a time to weep.
- God notices our tears; they are precious to him (Isaiah 38:3-5).

5. What helps us when we are grieving?

💬 DISCUSSION, IN SMALL GROUPS

1. When you have been mourning the loss of someone or something, what sort of helpful things have people done or said?
2. What sort of unhelpful things have people done or said?

What helps when we're grieving?

- People who listen to our pain, who do more listening than talking. We cannot absorb teaching and sermons at this time (Job 21:2; Proverbs 18:13).
- People who help us with practical things, at time of funeral but also in following months and years.
- Reminding ourselves that it is normal to grieve, and that it is a process that will take time. We will not always feel like we do today.
- Avoiding big decisions and major changes, like marrying someone. When we are in Camp 3, we will be able to make better decisions.
- Getting exercise and wearing ourselves out physically, so we can sleep better. It's common to have difficulty sleeping in the weeks and months after a loss.
- Reading the psalms, especially the laments. These can provide great comfort.
- Bringing our losses to the Lord, one by one. The more specific we can be, the better.

Laments

One of the tools we can use to help us grieve is lament. In a lament, people pour out their complaints to God and ask God to act on their behalf, often while stating their hope or trust in God.

Laments in the Bible can have the following parts.

- Address to God ("O God")
- Review of God's faithfulness in the past
- **A complaint**
- A confession of sin or claim of innocence
- A request for help
- God's response (often not stated)
- A vow to praise God or a statement of trust in God

Not all parts are present in each lament, and they are not always in the same order. The only essential part is the complaint.

A lament allows a person to fully express their grief and even accuse God, but this is often followed by a statement of trust in God. This combination makes for a very powerful prayer. The grief is not hidden, but the person does not stay in their grief—they call on God and try to express their trust. The laments encourage people be honest with God, to speak the truth about their feelings and doubts. To lament to God is a sign of faith, not doubt.

In a lament, people do not attempt to solve the problem themselves, but they cry to God for help. They look to God, not an enemy or random chance, as the one ultimately in control of the situation. They ask God to take action to bring justice rather than taking action themselves or cursing the enemy.

Psalm 13	Lament part
¹ How much longer will you forget me, LORD? Forever? How much longer will you hide yourself from me? ² How long must I endure trouble? How long will sorrow fill my heart day and night? How long will my enemies triumph over me?	Address and complaint
³ Look at me, O LORD my God, and answer me. Restore my strength; don't let me die. ⁴ Don't let my enemies say, "We have defeated him." Don't let them gloat over my downfall.	Request
⁵ I rely on your constant love;	Statement of trust in God
I will be glad, because you will rescue me. ⁶ I will sing to you, O LORD, because you have been good to me.	Vow to praise

*Sixty-seven of the Psalms are considered laments—more than any other type of psalm. Some were for use by individuals; others were used by the community together. The individual lament Psalms are: 3, 4, 5, 6, 7, 9-10, 11, 13, 16, 17, 22, 25, 26, 27, 28, 31, 35, 36, 38, 39, 40, 42, 43, 51, 52, 54, 55, 56, 57, 59, 61, 62, 63, 64, 69, 70, 71, 77, 86, 88, 94, 102, 109, 120, 130, 140, 141, 142, 143. The community lament Psalms are: 12, 14, 44, 53, 58, 60, 74, 79, 80, 83, 85, 90, 106, 108, 123, 126, 137.

» Write a lament

Take some time to create a lament to God. Read Psalm 13 as an example. Your lament could be a song, rap, poem, prayer, or any creative way you wish to express your feelings to God. It does not have to include all parts of a lament, but it does need to have a complaint.

Use this space or a separate sheet of paper to write your lament.

💬 DISCUSSION, IN SMALL GROUPS

Share as much or as little as you'd like of your lament. Or share what the process of writing a lament was like for you.

Taking care of yourself

It can be hard to go right back into your cell or unit after opening up so many strong emotions. Do the container exercise again to help you put some things "back in the box" until later, when you can process them more fully. You can also do the breathing exercise and the senses exercise.

What's one thing you will do to take care of yourself today?

Wrapping it up

What's one thing you want to remember from this lesson?

Voices

Lament of a Forgiven Son

Father you Created me, you Knew me Even when I was in my mothers womb. What a disappointment I must have been when you looked upon me, for from the beginning I suffered, from the moment I came into this world my life has been full of torment and pain. From my Fathers hand Death tried to seize me, pain and fear ruled my life til the age of fourteen—when truth from my mother's life set me free; Only to set me up for the next tramatic scene to Grip my Life, to riddle my hopes and Dreams, with agony and pain. Death to come in and take from me the only women I had and would ever Love, but not only my Queen but the child I longed to love, my "baby Girl" who I would never be able to hold-to-comfort in her time of fear—of a world filled with hatred and evil, to read to her and watch over her as she slept, to Laugh with her and when in pain, to cry with and Shield her as best I could from all Evil. Which til this Day the pain and agony of there memory Cripples me. I am stuck in my mind of what could and should have been. So I Replace Love with addiction and pain. Until the Death at my birth catches up with me, to write the mistake of my Fathers hand. For truly I wish i had died that day.

For what good is man, but to be fruitful and multiply. I have no wife, no heir, nothing to remind the world that I existed. So Lord what truly Did my birth accomplish. Why my Lord? Why Let me Live? End the pain which is my life.

My Lord Creator of heaven and earth Look down and have mercy on me for the trouble of my heart is heavy. If you dont help me truly the weight shall crush me. for my tears dont stop flowing and I am weak from sobbing. I cant eat for food no longer sustains me. There is no pleasure no taste in my mouth. The water I drink just feeds the tears of my heart. Help me Lord for I am tired and there is no rest for me.

Father God from the day of my youth I was taught of your Love and mercy, how it endurers forever, and how your love is always present. So I Shall still my heart and trust in you, for I know you are my savior my God and my King. And that the whole world is under your Dominion. I know you are a just God and that you hear the cries of your people. So I shall wait on you my Lord. for I know true Deliverance comes from you.

TAKING YOUR PAIN TO THE CROSS

Taking care of yourself

When we remember painful experiences, we need to stay aware of our bodies and to remind ourselves that we are no longer in the past. Consider using the breathing exercise or the senses exercise before starting this lesson.

Pain to the cross ceremony

We have taken time to recognize the pains we are carrying. We've expressed our pain by sharing and listening to one another, in laments, and in the art exercise. Now we will bring those pains to the cross where Jesus died and ask him to bring healing to our wounded hearts. We will do a ceremony where we write down the wounds of our hearts, then bring these wounds and pain to Jesus.

You may find this ceremony helpful. It will not necessarily heal all heart wounds instantaneously. You may need to bring your pain to Christ again many times in the healing process. You can do so in your thoughts and prayers, even in the middle of the night.

1. Identify the wounds of your heart

We are here to take our pain to the cross. We are taught in Scripture that Jesus came not only to bear our sins but also to bear our pain and heal us. In the Gospel according to Matthew we read: *"When evening came, people brought to Jesus many who had demons in them. Jesus drove out the evil spirits with a word and healed all who were sick. He did this to make come true what the prophet Isaiah had said, 'He himself took our sickness and carried away our diseases'"* (Matthew 8:16–17).

Matthew was quoting from the book of Isaiah, which says: "*We despised him and rejected him; he endured suffering and pain.... But he endured the suffering that should have been ours, the pain we should have borne. All the while we thought that his suffering was punishment sent by God*" (Isaiah 53:3-4).

In Luke 4 we learn that Jesus went to the synagogue and read aloud from the book of the prophet Isaiah: "*The Spirit of the Lord is upon me because he has chosen me to bring good news to the poor. He has sent me to proclaim liberty to the captives and recovery of sight to the blind, to set free the oppressed and announce that the time has come when the Lord will save his people*" (Luke 4:18-19).

We further learn that after reading this passage, "*Jesus rolled up the scroll, gave it to the attendant, and sat down. All the people in the synagogue had their eyes fixed on him as he said to them, 'This passage of scripture has come true today, as you heard it being read'*" (Luke 4:20-21).

Jesus felt the full burden of human pain and sinfulness. Jesus knows the pain that is in our hearts. We need to bring it to him so that he can heal us. In this exercise, we will bring our pain to the cross.

» Write down your worst pain

- Painful things that have been done to you.
- Painful things you have seen done to others, or bad dreams you have had.
- Painful things you have heard about that have happened to others.
- Painful things that you have done to others.

Write these things on another sheet of paper.

Share your pain.

💬 DISCUSSION

In small groups, share as much or as little as you wish of what you wrote down, or share what the process of writing it down was like. Listen without criticizing or offering advice. Share openly but don't dwell on violent parts. Pray for each other if you feel comfortable doing so.

2. Bring your wounds and pain to Jesus

Isaiah 53:4-6 says:
> But he endured the suffering that should have been ours,
> the pain that we should have borne.
> All the while we thought that his suffering
> was punishment sent by God.
> But because of our sins he was wounded,
> beaten because of the evil we did.
> We are healed by the punishment he suffered,
> made whole by the blows he received.
> All of us were like sheep that were lost,
> each of us going his own way.
> But the Lord made the punishment fall on him,
> the punishment all of us deserved.

Talk to Jesus about your pain.

Take some time to bring your pain to Jesus. Tell him exactly what it is—anger, sadness, loneliness, feeling abandoned. Try to let out all the pain and emotions you feel about your loss or hurt.

Bring your pain to the cross.
Say (out loud if possible), "I'm handing over my suffering to Jesus, who died on the cross for me."

Destroy the papers.

Isaiah 61:1-3 says:

> The Sovereign LORD has filled me with his Spirit.
> He has chosen me and sent me
> to bring good news to the poor,
> to heal the broken-hearted,
> to announce release to captives
> and freedom to those in prison.
> He has sent me to proclaim that the time has come
> when the Lord will save his people
> and defeat their enemies.
> He has sent me to comfort all who mourn,
> to give to those who mourn in Zion
> joy and gladness instead of grief,
> a song of praise instead of sorrow.
> They will be like trees
> that the LORD himself has planted.
> They will all do what is right,
> and God will be praised for what he has done.

Taking care of yourself

Remembering the most painful things in your life takes a lot of courage and energy. It is normal to feel more tired or emotional than usual, or to have difficulty sleeping. Don't be discouraged. Recognize and celebrate the ways you have been courageous.

Remember the exercises you've learned to cope with strong emotions. Before you leave, consider doing the breathing exercise or the senses exercise.

What's one thing you will do to take care of yourself today?

Wrapping it up

What's one thing you want to remember from this lesson?

Voices

December 12, 2016

When I walked into the class room at Douglas County Corrections, at age 56, I was facing my (4) fourth prison number and a parole violation from my (3) third prison number.

The scars were so deeply hidden—I could not verbally express them

Struck down by physical abuse of the body, I thought it was no cure. My life was chaotic, and out of control. You feel ungodly when ungodly things happen to you. I was hurt—hopeless—it was too hard to move on.

I started stuffing instead of forgiving. I ran from one pain to find another.

Where is the comfort, and peace I once knew in God.

What is this pain thats holding me back from the blessed life I deserve to live. My emotions can not cope with the pain

The drugs could not numb the pain. The alcohol could not drown the pain. The abcess had made a hole so deep and ugly in my heart.

How could God heal me? Physically. Emotionally. Spiritually Exhausted.

How can the wounds of the heart heal

Walking in the class room—My God gave me the strength to talk about the trauma (the core of my pain).

I talked—I cried, I grieved, got mad

I called on God, and shared my complaints. I asked for help, and trusted in His Power. The soothing oil from Jesus poured over me, as I nailed my pain to the cross.

I have seen my own brokeness, and given every shattered piece to God. Through His grace and mercy—Praise honor and glory belong to Him. God snatched me out—before I fell in deep depression

He knows me better than anyone. I don't have to keep exhausting myself trying to rebuild my life after another shipwreck.

He controls the storm.

Through his grace and mercy I see a new vision. I see the others, the 97% of women who suffer trauma, and don't know it.

Now I have an eye to see the other's and extend a helping hand.

The grace to step outside myself.

HOW CAN WE FORGIVE OTHERS?

Taking care of yourself

There are things we can do when we're not stressed, to help ourselves cope when we are stressed. It's like packing for a road trip—you don't need things now, but you will need them later. If you have time, try the tree exercise on page 65.

1. Forgiveness skits

Think about the forgiveness skits you saw or participated in. (1) "There is nothing to forgive." (2) "Until you forget, you haven't forgiven." (3) "I forgive you for the hurt you caused me."

DISCUSSION

1. Which of these situations show real forgiveness?
2. How is it different from the others?

2. Forgiveness is not …

Forgiveness is not	Forgiveness is

Forgiveness is not ...

- Saying the offense didn't matter or that we were not hurt by what the person did.
- Being able to make sense of why the person did what he or she did.
- Acting as if the event never happened.
- Dependent on the offender apologizing first or changing their behavior.
- Letting those who do wrong avoid the consequences of their action.
- Letting the offender hurt us or other innocent people again.
- Trusting a person again right after they hurt us.

3. How can we forgive others?

If we think forgiving is too hard for us to do, we are right. God is the only one who can enable us to forgive (1 Peter 2:24).

Bring the pain to Christ.
Forgiving someone begins when we recognize that the person has wronged us and we accept the pain their sin has caused us. To say it has not hurt if it did is to lie, and we are called to speak the truth (Ephesians 4:25). We bring our pain to the cross and release it to Jesus. When Jesus heals our pain, then we will be able to forgive those who have hurt us.

Do not wait for the other person to apologize.
Often we are unwilling to forgive until the offender has apologized to us. Or we want to see that the person has changed their behavior before we forgive them. Like Jesus, we need to forgive people, even if they are not sorry about the evil they have done (Romans 5:8). On the cross he said, "Forgive them, Father! They don't know what they are doing" (Luke 23:34).

Allow time for the process.

Offense → Complete Forgiveness

When we forgive someone, we will still remember what happened. At first, we may still feel the pain associated with it. When this happens, we need to continue to take the parts that hurt to Jesus. The commitment to forgive often comes before the feelings of forgiveness, and sometimes long before. As we bring our hurt to Jesus over and over, eventually we will feel less pain when we remember the event.

Let wrongdoers face the consequences of their actions.

Forgiving someone does not mean that they will not be punished if they have done wrong things. By forgiving, we allow God to judge and take revenge (Romans 12:19).

God uses the authorities to deal with those who break the law (Romans 13:1-4). Even though we have forgiven someone, it may be necessary to bring them to justice to prevent others from being hurt in the future. Forgiveness does not mean the offender is excused from paying back what was taken (Numbers 5:5-7).

💬 DISCUSSION

What are some common sayings about forgiveness in our society? How do they compare with what the Bible tells us?

4. Why does God want us to forgive other people?

Consider the following verses:

- Ephesians 4:26-27
- 2 Corinthians 2:10-11
- Hebrews 12:14-15
- 1 John 4:10
- Ephesians 4:32
- Matthew 18:21-35

Forgiveness frees us from anger and bitterness.
- When we are angry, we can give Satan a foothold in our hearts (Ephesians 4:26-27).
- Refusing to forgive can make us physically ill. It may make us become as violent and evil as those who offended us. Forgiveness releases us from all this. We forgive for our own good (2 Corinthians 2:10-11).
- If we do not forgive others, we pass our hatred on to our children, resulting in cycles of revenge and violence between groups which can go on for generations, poisoning people (Hebrews 12:14-15).

Forgiveness shows that we understand Christ's sacrifice and our salvation.
- When we understand how much we have offended God by our sinfulness, and how Jesus offered himself for our forgiveness even before we repented (1 John 4:10), any offense we have experienced will seem small.
- We will want to extend that same forgiveness to others (Ephesians 4:32; Matthew 18:21-35).

Forgiveness allows us to be reconciled with those who have offended us.
- Until we forgive those who have offended us, our relationship with them will suffer.
- Forgiveness makes it possible for our relationship with them to be restored.
- Full restoration, however, requires repentance and forgiveness by both parties.

Forgiveness can sometimes change the person who offended us.
- Forgiving someone may be the start of God bringing that person to repentance.
- In Acts 7, as Stephen was dying, he forgave those who were killing him. One of those people was Saul, who later became Paul the apostle (Acts 7:59—8:1).

💬 DISCUSSION, IN SMALL GROUPS

1. What do you find the hardest thing about forgiving someone?

2. What has helped you the most to forgive others?

5. What if we are the ones who have caused the offense?

We need to repent ...

- Allow God's Spirit to show us how much our sin hurts God and others (James 4:8-9; 2 Corinthians 7:10).
- Take responsibility for what we have done and clearly state our sin (Proverbs 28:13; Psalm 32:3-5).
- Seek God's forgiveness of our sin, and then accept that God has done so (1 John 1:9).
- Ask those we've offended to forgive us, without excusing ourselves, blaming them, or demanding that they trust us again right away (James 5:16).
- Show our repentance by the way we act (Acts 26:20b).
- If possible, pay back what was taken (Numbers 5:5-7).

» Forgiveness exercise

If you need to forgive someone:

Write down the name of a person (or people) you need to forgive. Use a symbol to represent the person if you are concerned about privacy:

What do you need to forgive them for?

How did their actions make you feel?

Pray: "God, I forgive *[or, please help me to forgive]* _____ for doing _____ .

It made me feel _____."

If you need to be forgiven for harm you have done:

I need to ask _____ to forgive me.

What harm did you do to them?

How might you have made them feel?

Pray: "God, please forgive me for doing _____ to _____. Please help me do the things that show I have repented."

What plans can you make to ask the person you hurt for forgiveness?

If we confess our sins to God, he will keep his promise and do what is right: he will forgive us our sins and purify us from all our wrongdoing. (1 John 1:9)

Taking care of yourself

Take a moment to see how you are feeling now. Do you need to do a breathing exercise or the senses exercise? What's one thing you can do to take care of yourself today?

Wrapping it up

What's one thing you want to remember from this lesson?

Voices

Things started off rough in my life from the very beginning. My dad was a violent alcoholic and my older brother and I witnessed a lot of abuse with my father beating my mother. When my mother was pregnant with me, my dad held my brother and mother hostage at gun point. Violence was a constant occurrence in our home until age four, when they finally divorced. Our lives became normal enough after that. I lived with my mom and I got a good step dad. I had friends and we played Barbie; I liked sports. Our family went together to the Catholic Church. Things became pretty normal.

My brother, however, always seemed to be in trouble and my parent's full attention was on him. Like my dad, he was very violent not only to family members but would tear up the house in his rages. They were always correcting and disciplining him until finally one day, they gave him over to the state. I think this is when I remember the shift happening in our family. I felt a sense of uneasiness that my parents would give up on him. I got the feeling that if I did enough wrong, they would give me up as well. Also at this time with my brother gone, all of their attentions turned in my direction. That correction and discipline they had used on my brother was suddenly focused on me. From the age of 10 to age 18 my mom, with the help of my step dad, would hold me down and spank me like a little child when I did wrong. I felt humiliation with this and really hated being restrained by my step dad. I began seething with anger.

I had always done well in school. I was a good student, a cheerleader, and even received a college scholarship in cheerleading, and I was active in sports. I did, however, still have a huge amount of anger built up inside of me. I learned to release it by fighting. Usually on a weekly basis, matches would be arranged in a field for me and a large number of kids from our small town, 60 to 80, would gather to watch me fight. This was the only way I knew how to release my building, internal rage.

One time when I was about 15, my mother drug tested me and discovered that I tested positive for pot. To punish me my step-dad held me down so my mom could spank me. He had on a robe and I could feel his unclothed body under the robe up against my skin. I was screaming for him to get off me but he kept holding me down. Out of desperation I bit him. My parents' response was to call the police and let me sit in jail for five days. They then kicked me out of the house. I ended up losing all my scholarships for college as I scrambled to live life on my own. It was at this time that I started using cocaine, alcohol, and eventually crack.

During the process of all of this chaos, I had two beautiful children. Sadly, I raised them with this explosive anger and they experienced many things children should not see.

I was arrested in March 2016 on an assault charge. The night before I was arrested I had been in a fight with my boyfriend and threw my cell phone at him so hard that I cracked his skull. While in jail I caught an additional assault on a woman who I had cut with a knife and brutally beat. I was in once again in jail full of anger, hatred, and rage. I was like a bomb ready to explode.

It was during my jail stay that I heard about this class on trauma healing. I was asked to sign up. I not only came to faith in Christ during this class but God brought this entire trauma in my life to the forefront. I had no idea that the trauma of my childhood was the underlying factor in my anger. It was always under the surface ready to explode but the class taught me how to deal with it. I was taught how to deal with it by writing laments, talking, and bringing it to the cross and eventually forgiveness. I know now that if I did not let God heal the trauma, I would be back in jail on another assault charge.

When I first came to jail, I was often locked down for fighting. That was who I was. But after taking the class and getting to the root of my anger, I have since walked away from countless encounters. One day the chaplain who taught the trauma class was in the housing unit and was able to witness first hand the change that has taken place in my life. I had an inmate try to verbally provoke a physical fight with me. She was in my face, being physically aggressive, screaming obscenities. Oh, my old behavior would have unleashed on this woman but I was able to put both my hands in the air, walk away, and go to my cell. The women even followed after me with taunts but I no longer felt the need to fight.

I see so many women in jail come in and out and in again whose hearts are overflowing with pain. There are so many who have unresolved trauma in their lives. My desire is to first go back to be a loving mom with my kids in Colorado but eventually go into the jail and conduct trauma healing classes. These classes have truly changed my life.

LOOKING BACK

In this final section you will find three ways of thinking about your life and your struggles that may help you see your life story differently. You'll also find an exercise to help you take care of yourself on the journey.

1. How does God use suffering?

DISCUSSION
1. How has God used suffering in your life?
2. Read the following verses and discuss how God has used suffering in people's lives:
    - 1 Peter 1:6-7
    - Genesis 50:18-20
    - Isaiah 40:11
    - 2 Corinthians 1:3-5.

2. The healing journey

Take another look at the healing journey diagram. We have learned several steps of the process of healing from heart wounds—expressing our pain through words and art, grieving, lamenting, bringing our pain to the cross, and forgiving. As we continue to practice these steps, we will be able to rebuild our lives and be better able to face suffering in the future. We will have good days and bad days—it's all part of the journey. And as we learned in this group, we can talk to God at every step.

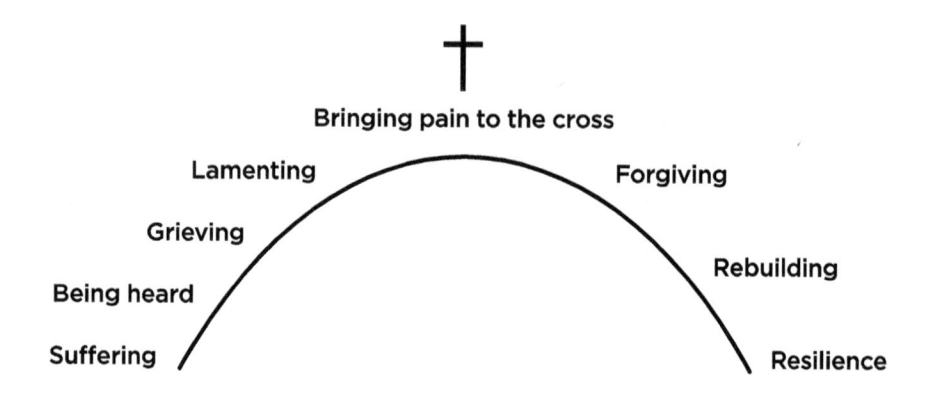

†
Bringing pain to the cross

Lamenting   Forgiving

Grieving

                                Rebuilding

Being heard

Suffering   Resilience

Taking care of yourself

This exercise can help us build the ability to handle tough situations and emotions and prepare our mind for future conflict.

» *Tree exercise*

Read Psalm 1:1-3a.

> Happy are those who reject the advice of evil people,
> who do not follow the example of sinners
> or join those who have no use for God.
>
> Instead, they find joy in obeying the Law of the LORD,
> and they study it day and night.
>
> They are like trees that grow beside a stream,
> that bear fruit at the right time,
> and whose leaves do not dry up.

Now fix your eyes in one place or, if you're comfortable, close your eyes. Imagine that you are a tree.

- What kind of tree would you be? See yourself as that kind of tree.
- In your imagination, look around. Is your tree by itself?
- What's the landscape around you?

Now look at the trunk of the tree.

- Notice it going down into the earth and up into the branches. Follow the branches way out into the leaves. (If it's a fruit tree, see the fruit hanging from the branches.)

Now follow the trunk down to the roots.

- Look at the roots—is it a long single root or many roots going out? Notice how the roots are anchored into the ground.
- Now watch how the root system is bringing water and nutrients to the roots and how those nutrients travel up the tree to the branches.

Notice the weather.

- Imagine the sun shining on the leaves, making oxygen. Imagine the tree just being there in just the right temperature and light.
- Now the tree needs a bit of water. Imagine a gentle rain slowly coming down over the leaves and going towards the roots. See the water going down, down into the roots. See the moisture being taken up into the tree.
- Now stop the rain; see the sun coming out to dry the leaves.

Now imagine the tree with some live creatures—perhaps birds, or squirrels or insects going up and down. Watch all the activity.

Now there's a storm.

- Black clouds are beginning to form in the distance. The storm won't harm or destroy the tree but the storm will come.
- The wind is picking up and the clouds are coming. The branches are shaking. The trunk is moving back and forth. Some of the leaves are falling and some of the fruit is falling.
- Now focus on how the roots are holding firm and allowing the tree to move back and forth in the wind. Let the storm go on a bit. Feel the tree moving back and forth with its roots firmly planted in the ground.
- Now the storm is slowing gradually until everything is still again.
- How is the tree feeling after the storm?
- Now the sun is returning. The insects and birds are coming back out again.
- Things are drying. Imagine the tree coming back to normal.
- When the tree is still again, the sun is shining, and the insects and the birds are back out again, gradually take some deep breaths and open your eyes.

ON YOUR OWN

The final pages of this journal are for you. Do you have a story of healing? Do you have something you want to share with God?

CPSIA information can be obtained
at www.ICGtesting.com
Printed in the USA
JSHW082226071122
32806JS00003B/188